Animals at the Pond

Élisabeth de Lambilly-Bresson

GARETH**STEVENS**

GS

PUBLISHING

A Member of the WRC Media Family of Companies

The Frog

I am a frog.
You can hear me
croaking near the pond.
"Ribbet! Ribbet! Ribbet!"
But if you try to catch me,
I quickly jump away!

The Dragonfly

I am a dragonfly.
I am a dancer
dressed in shiny,
see-through wings.
Lightly and gracefully,
I twirl around the pond.

The Carp

I am a carp.
I hide in the dark
at the bottom of the pond.
If you wait and watch,
you might see me swim
to the top of the water
to swallow a tasty insect.
Gulp!

The Heron

I am a heron.
My skinny legs are so strong,
I balance on one at a time.
I stand high above the pond
and quietly watch for fish.
I catch them with one stab
of my long, sharp beak.

The Swan

I am a swan.
I am proud
of my silky white feathers.
Gliding across the water,
I am the queen of the pond.
I bend my long neck gracefully
to find food in the cool water.

The Nutria

I am a nutria.
I look a lot like a rat,
but I live on the pond
like a beaver.
I build a raft on the water
or dig a safe burrow
near the pond.

The Kingfisher

I am a kingfisher.
When it comes to
spotting and catching fish,
I am the king.
That is how I got my name!
Each day, I perch
high above the pond,
looking for my lunch.

14

Please visit our Web site at: www.garethstevens.com
For a free color catalog describing Gareth Stevens Publishing's
list of high-quality books and multimedia programs, call
1-800-542-2595 (USA) or 1-800-387-3178 (Canada).
Gareth Stevens Publishing's fax: (414) 332-3567.

Library of Congress Cataloging-in-Publication Data

Lambilly-Bresson, Elisabeth de
   [Au bord de l'étang. English]
   Animals at the pond / Elisabeth de Lambilly-Bresson. — North American ed.
      p. cm. — (Animal show and tell)
   ISBN-13: 978-0-8368-7830-1 (lib. bdg.)
   1. Pond animals—Juvenile literature. I. Title.
QL146.3.L3613   2007
591.763'6—dc22   2006032928

This edition first published in 2007 by
Gareth Stevens Publishing
A Member of the WRC Media Family of Companies
330 West Olive Street, Suite 100
Milwaukee, WI 53212 USA

Translation: Gini Holland
Gareth Stevens editor: Gini Holland
Gareth Stevens art direction and design: Tammy West

This edition copyright © 2007 by Gareth Stevens, Inc. Original edition copyright
© 2002 by Mango Jeunesse Press. First published as *Les animinis:
Au bord de l'étang* by Mango Jeunesse Press.

Printed in the United States of America

1 2 3 4 5 6 7 8 9 10 10 09 08 07 06